PAYDAY!

Lemonade 50¢

MONEY MATTERS

Earning Money

by Mari Schuh

BLASTOFF! READERS 2

BELLWETHER MEDIA • MINNEAPOLIS, MN

Note to Librarians, Teachers, and Parents:

Blastoff! Readers are carefully developed by literacy experts and combine standards-based content with developmentally appropriate text.

Level 1 provides the most support through repetition of high-frequency words, light text, predictable sentence patterns, and strong visual support.

Level 2 offers early readers a bit more challenge through varied simple sentences, increased text load, and less repetition of high-frequency words.

Level 3 advances early-fluent readers toward fluency through increased text and concept load, less reliance on visuals, longer sentences, and more literary language.

Level 4 builds reading stamina by providing more text per page, increased use of punctuation, greater variation in sentence patterns, and increasingly challenging vocabulary.

Level 5 encourages children to move from "learning to read" to "reading to learn" by providing even more text, varied writing styles, and less familiar topics.

Whichever book is right for your reader, Blastoff! Readers are the perfect books to build confidence and encourage a love of reading that will last a lifetime!

This edition first published in 2016 by Bellwether Media, Inc.

No part of this publication may be reproduced in whole or in part without written permission of the publisher. For information regarding permission, write to Bellwether Media, Inc., Attention: Permissions Department, 5357 Penn Avenue South, Minneapolis, MN 55419.

Library of Congress Cataloging-in-Publication Data

Schuh, Mari C., 1975-
  Earning Money / by Mari Schuh.
    pages cm. – (Blastoff! Readers: Money Matters)
  Summary: "Relevant images match informative text in this introduction to earning money. Intended for students in kindergarten through third grade"– Provided by publisher.
  Audience: Ages 5-8
  Audience: K to grade 3
  Includes bibliographical references and index.
  ISBN 978-1-62617-246-3 (hardcover: alk. paper)
  1. Money–Juvenile literature. 2. Wages–Juvenile literature. I. Title.
  HG221.5.S377 2016
  650.1'2–dc23
                              2015006566

Printed in the United States of America, North Mankato, MN.

Table of Contents

Why Earn Money?

Why must people have money?

People use money to pay for their **needs**. Money buys food and clothes.

COMMON NEEDS

food

clothes

school supplies

shoes

People also use money
to pay for their **wants**.

COMMON WANTS

toys

sweets

games

movies

They spend it on fun toys and tasty sweets.

Ways to Earn Money

People work to earn money. Kids rake leaves, wash cars, and babysit younger kids.

Some kids earn money from their parents. They earn an **allowance** for helping out at home.

They take out the trash.
They wash dishes after dinner.

Some people sell used or handmade things to earn money. They sell these items at yard sales or on web sites.

Kids earn money by selling lemonade. They sell fresh cookies at bake sales.

Using Earned Money

People save, spend, or give away the money they earn.

Kids often save their
money in a piggy bank.
They can spend it later.

People spend their money on **goods**. They buy books, shoes, and more.

People also spend their money on **services**. They get a haircut or have their car fixed.

Sometimes people **donate** some of their earned money. They give it to **charities** and to people in need.

CHARITY

Most people keep some money in a **savings account** at a **bank**.

The money grows because it earns **interest**. Then people have even more money!

Glossary

allowance—money paid to someone at regular times; many kids earn an allowance every week.

bank—a business where people keep their money

charities—groups that raise money to help people in need

donate—to give something away

goods—things that can be bought and sold

interest—money that is paid to people for keeping their money in a bank account, savings bond, or other account

needs—things people must have to live, such as food, clothes, and a place to live

savings account—a bank account that pays people interest for keeping their money in it

services—work that helps others

wants—things people would like to have, such as games, toys, and treats

To Learn More

AT THE LIBRARY

Bullard, Lisa. *Ella Earns Her Own Money.*
Minneapolis, Minn.: Millbrook Press, 2014.

Reina, Mary. *Earn Money.* North Mankato, Minn.:
Capstone Press, 2015.

Schwartz, Heather E. *Earn Wisely.* Mankato, Minn.:
Amicus, 2016.

ON THE WEB

Learning more about earning
money is as easy as 1, 2, 3.

1. Go to www.factsurfer.com.

2. Enter "earning money" into the search box.

3. Click the "Surf" button and you will see a
   list of related web sites.

With factsurfer.com, finding more
information is just a click away.

Index